FILL IN THE GAPS 4

by
Edward R. Rosset

Editorial Stanley

Written by
Edward R. Rosset
Member of the Bachelor of Arts Association
of Euskadi.

Revised by
Beryl Aguado Lait
Principal of Apsley School of English.
Portsmouth - England

Published by
Editorial Stanley

Layout
Angela Gómez Martín

Front page design
Esquema

Apdo. 207 - 20302 IRUN - SPAIN
Telf. (943) 64 04 12 - Fax. (943) 64 38 63

ISBN: 84-7873-278-0
Dep. Leg.: BI- 653-99

First edition 1995
Second edition 1999

Printers
Imprenta RGM

FILL IN THE GAPS 2

Fill in the gaps 2

PAGES **CONTENTS**

Fill in the gaps 2

WHAT A/AN · WHAT · HOW

1. '.................... nice girl Jennifer is!' 'Yes, ... nice she is!
2. .... horrible houses those are! .... horrible those houses are!
3. .... stupid you were to lose your passport! .... a stupid boy you are!
4. .... awful weather we are having these days. .... horrible the weather is!
5. .... horrible houses those are! .... horrible those houses are!
6. .... attractive face that little girl has! .... attractive it is!
7. .... horrible news this is! .... terrible piece of news!
8. My God! .... horrible coffee that woman makes! .... horrible it is!
9. .... difficult the problem was! .... difficult problem that was!
10. Heavens! .... meal! It is terrible! .... terrible this meal is!
11. .... heavy these suitcases are! .... heavy suitcases these are!
12. .... wonderful girls those are! .... wonderful those girls are!
13. .... big and beautiful this mansion is! .... big mansion this is!
14. .... good teachers you have in this school! .... good these teachers are!
15. .... nice that Mercedes car is! .... nice Mercedes car that is!
16. .... exciting adventure that is! .... exciting that adventure is!
17. .... nuisance. We have to walk all the way to the petrol station!
18. .... nonsense is this? .... lot of rubbish that is!
19. .... stupid I was to say that I had made a mistake! .... stupid fool I was!
20. .... irresponsible he was to drive without a driving licence. .... irresponsible fool he was!

21. .... honest he was to say that he had copied the exam! .... honest boy he is!

22. .... waste of time this is, playing cards all day! .... silly it is to waste the time like this!

23. .... pity, we are not going to arrive in time for the first race.

24. .... shame! He couldn't get there in time to save the poor cat.

25. .... lucky your were to win the prize! .... lucky man you are!

26. .... wide this road is! .... wide road this is!

27. .... long queues there are for the buses! .... long those queues are!

28. .... terrible beer this is! .... terrible this beer is!

29. .... untidy this room is! .... untidy room this is!

30. .... idiot that girl is! .... stupid that girl is!

31. .... awful speech he made last night! .... awful it was!

32. .... fantastic bargain I found yesterday! .... fantastic this bargain is!

33. .... lot of money that woman has! .... rich she is!

34. Look at that doll, ... lovely it is! .... lovely doll it is!

35. .... beautiful that sweater is! .... beautiful sweater that is!

36. .... funny haircut you've got, Jimmy! .... funny that haircut looks!

37. .... awful wind we are having! .... awful this wind is!

38. .... meal! It's terrible! .... terrible meal! .... terrible this meal is!

39. .... terrible books those are! .... terrible those books are!

40. .... nice the Browns' children are! .... nice children the Browns have.

Fill in the gaps 2

SUCH · SUCH A · SO

1. Johnny is .... nice little boy! He and his brother are .... nice!
2. The Browns' children are .... intelligent! They are .... intelligent children!
3. These books are .... terrible! They are .... terrible books!
4. It is .... impressive building! That building is .... impressive!
5. Little Johnny is .... stupid boy! That boy is .... stupid!
6. We are having .... horrible weather these days! The weather is .... horrible these days!
7. Those houses are .... terrible! They are .... terrible houses!
8. That child has .... attractive little face! Her face is .... attractive!
9. Today the news is .... terrible! Today there is .... terrible news!
10. The coffee you make is .... incredibly bad! You make .... bad coffee!
11. We've got .... terrible problem at home! The problem we've got is .... terrible!
12. We had .... wonderful meal! The meal we had was .... wonderful!
13. The suitcase was .... heavy that I couldn't lift it! It was .... heavy suitcase!
14. Those girls are .... beautiful! They are .... beautiful girls!
15. They live in .... big mansion that you can get lost in it! The mansion is .... big!
16. The teachers we have at school are .... good! We have .... good teachers!
17. Americans have .... large cars! American cars are .... large!
18. The adventure was .... exciting! It was .... exciting adventure!
19. It is .... nuisance to have to get up so early!
20. He's talking rubbish. I never heard .... nonsense in all my life!

21. That boy is .... stupid fool! He is .... stupid!

22. He is .... irresponsible driving without a licence! He is .... irresponsible man!

23. He is .... honest man! This man is .... honest!

24. It is .... waste of time to copy all that! It is .... silly to waste time like that!

25. It was .... pity that we couldn't get there in time to hear it!

26. It was .... shame that he couldn't finish it in time for the congress!

27. You are .... lucky man to win the first prize! You were .... lucky!

28. Motorways are .... comfortable in this country! You have .... comfortable motorways here!

29. There's .... long queue to buy tickets for the concert! The queue is .... long!

30. You have .... horrible beer in this country! The beer is .... horrible here!

31. Those boys have .... untidy bedrooms! Those boys' bedrooms are .... untidy!

32. That boy is .... idiot! That boy is .... stupid!

33. The president made .... awful speech last night! The speech he made was .... awful!

34. I found .... fantastic bargain yesterday! The bargain I found yesterday was .... fantastic!

35. That old woman has .... lot of money! That old woman is .... rich!

36. That little girl has .... lovely doll! That doll is .... lovely!

37. This skirt is .... lovely! It is .... lovely skirt!

38. Your hairstyle is .... funny! You've got .... funny hairstyle!

39. We are having .... terrible winds! These winds we are having are .... terrible!

40. It was .... incredible piece of news that we couldn't believe it! The news was .... incredible!

Fill in the gaps 2

SUBJUNCTIVE

1. You're very small. If you .... taller you could be a policeman! (be)
2. Even if you .... you won't be able to do it properly. (want)
3. I wish I .... what to do in a situation like this! (know)
4. I'm not sure, darling, but I may .... a coat this afternoon. (buy)
5. The next time I .... to London I'll bring you a present. (go)
6. If you .... I could show you the museum next Saturday. (want)
7. I think that it is about time he .... to look after himself. (learn)
8. We really enjoyed the evening, but I think it's time we .... (go)
9. People were shouting everywhere 'Long .... the Queen' and 'God .... the Queen'. (live) (save)
10. He behaves as though he .... the owner of the place. (be)
11. He behaves as though he .... the whole place. (own)
12. My god! Heaven .... us if that man comes here! (help)
13. Your friend talked as if he .... where the missing girl was. (know)
14. He looked as though he .... a decent meal for months. (have)
15. If I .... rich I would live in a big mansion with many servants. (be)
16. If he .... to tell us everything, we could try to solve the problem. (be)
17. I should be a bit more careful about that if I .... you. (be)
18. We insist that a meeting .... as soon as possible. (hold)
19. It is vital that he .... before it is too late. (warn)
20. It is essential that every child .... the same educational opportunities.

21. He said it was important that every member .... his subscription by the end of June. (send)

22. I wish .... a flight to New York this afternoon! (there to be)

23. If only I .... there when she needed me! (be)

24. If I .... my rifle here I would kill that mad elephant. (have)

25. What would you do if you .... the president of the country? (be)

26. I know it's very small but I don't think it .... as small as they say. (be)

27. I wish Mummy .... us a story before going to bed tonight! (tell)

28. I wish he .... to see me soon! I can't wait to see him! (come)

29. If only that woman .... away and never returned! (go)

30. I think it's about time you .... some work this morning, boys! (do)

31. Before the boy left his home his father said to him: 'God .... you my son'. (bless)

32. That old man speaks as if he .... where the stolen money was. (know)

33. If I .... in your shoes I'd be looking for a flight to the other end of the world. (be)

34. They insisted that a solution .... as soon as possible. (find)

35. It is important that every man .... the same opportunities. (have)

36. If only you .... tell me the answer to that question! (to be able)

37. It is vital that we .... before the enemy comes to the bridge. (warn)

38. If I .... enough money I would pay you what I owe you. (have)

39. If I .... you I would be much more careful with the company I keep. (be)

40. I wish that woman .... playing the piano. She's getting on my nerves. (stop)

Fill in the gaps 2

CAN · COULD · MAY · MIGHT · SHOULD · OUGHT TO · MUST · NEED · DARE

1. Don't you think that you .... write to your father more often?
2. Your brother .... come next weekend. He said that he .... get a weekend pass.
3. I think that you .... smoke so much. You .... stop smoking.
4. ' .... I come in, Mr. Brown or are you busy?' 'You .... come in, of course.'
5. This old piano .... to be sold. It .... be kept in the attic. (ought) (should)
6. I will go early, otherwise he .... get angry. He gets furious when I am late.
7. You .... pay now. You .... pay later.
8. ' .... you speak English when you were a child?' 'No, I .... '
9. 'Where do you think he is?' 'Well, he .... be in London or Paris or New York - nobody knows.'
10. 'When are you coming?' 'I .... come tomorrow if I have time.'
11. 'Mary told me that your husband is ill. You .... have told me!'
12. It .... be too late. They .... have consulted a doctor earlier.
13. Jimmy, you .... speak with your mouth full. You .... finish what you have in your mouth before speaking.
14. I .... be in my office at nine o'clock every day of the week.
15. 'Jennifer hasn't arrived yet.' 'Well, her car .... have broken down.'
16. 'Somebody called. I think it was John.' 'It .... have been John, he's in the Antarctic.'
17. Well, I think you .... be so pessimistic, you .... be lucky.'
18. I'll say goodbye now. We .... meet again - who knows!
19. You .... have paid straight away. You .... have paid later.
20. You were crazy to drive like that, you .... have killed yourself.

CAN · COULD · MAY · MIGHT · SHOULD · OUGHT TO · MUST · NEED · DARE

21. How .... you speak to me like that, little boy! How .... you break in like that!

22. '.......... you understand what he is saying?' 'No, I .... understand him at all.'

23. I .... never run a marathon in three hours.

24. If it hadn't been for that they .... have reached the injured man before nightfall.

25. The lecture .... be understood by anyone present.

26. It .... be quite cold in Morrocco in January when I lived there.

27. You .... say those things about your teachers. You .... be more respectful.

28. All motorists .... to wear safety belts. They .... drive without them.

29. 'What shall we have for dinner on Sunday?' 'Well, we .... have roast lamb.'

30. You .... get up so early today, you know. It's Sunday.

31. You .... go to the bank for a loan. I .... lend you the money.

32. You .... have heard the explosion. It was deafening!

33. You .... have known my address by now. You have written to me a dozen times.

34. 'The Browns haven't arrived yet.' 'Well, they .... have been held up by traffic.'

35. We .... have been at the station when the train arrived.

36. He .... sing because he had a sore throat and he wasn't feeling well.

37. We have plenty of time. You .... have come so early.

38. She doesn't know yet, but she .... do a secretarial course next year.

39. It .... not be a bad thing if we took a holiday next week.

40. 'You .... have seen the match. It was smashing.' 'Yes, I .... to have gone.'

COMPARISON OF ADJECTIVES AND ADVERBS

1. Sorry, but this car is very small. We need a much .... one.
2. I'm afraid this shirt is far too big for me. Do you have a .... one?
3. We can go by car if there are four or five of us. It's so much .... We'll only pay for the petrol.
4. I have two sons. The .... is studying in the U.S.A. . The other one is still at school.
5. You speak too fast for me. Can you speak a bit .... ?
6. 'The situation is much .... than we thought.' 'Yes, it's very serious.'
7. Sylvia lives too far away! If she lived .... we could see each other more often.
8. 'It's much .... to learn Spanish in Spain than in London.' 'Yes, I agree it's not so difficult.'
9. Your daughter Margaret looks much .... today. Yesterday she was looking very sad.
10. It's very cold in the kitchen. It's .... in the sitting-room with the heater on.
11. This girl speaks French much .... than a year ago. She's learning fast.
12. 'It's much .... to learn a language as a child.' 'Yes, it's not so difficult.'
13. 'Will you drive ...., please? I'm afraid.' 'Well, I'm not driving fast.'
14. In the cellar of the house it's much .... than in the attic. It's very cold down there.
15. This girl is much .... than the winner of the beauty contest. She should have entered.
16. The Browns have two daughters. The .... is at university already. The other one is still at school.
17. The 'au pair' girl, Carmen, speaks English much .... than a year ago. She speaks very fluently now.
18. This house is much .... than the one we saw yesterday. That one wasn't very big.
19. Eating at home is much .... than going to a restaurant. In a restaurant it's very expensive.
20. This game isn't complicated. It's .... than you think.

COMPARISON OF ADJECTIVES AND ADVERBS

21. Our house is much .... away than yours. We still have to walk another mile.

22. .... to our telephone conversation I should like to place the following order.

23. I feel much .... today than yesterday. Yesterday I wasn't feeling very well.

24. If you spoke .... I would understand you much better. Don't speak so fast.

25. This book is boring. I am going to get a .... one.

26. This little girl is much .... than those. Those aren't very pretty.

27. If you had a map you would find your way much .... You wouldn't get lost.

28. That woman, Mrs. Robins, is much .... than she looks. She doesn't look very old.

29. Learning something is much .... than having a good time.

30. You know this town much .... than I do. I don't know it very well.

31. Ours is bad, but yours is much .... Yours is very bad indeed.

32. We can't go on talking any .... It is useless to talk any more.

33. Errol is my .... brother. He is four years .... than me. He is 20 and I'm 16.

34. This girl is only18, but her boyfriend is much .... He is 27.

35. 'Do you feel ....?' 'No, on the contrary, I feel much .... I feel horrible.'

36. This affair is much .... than I thought. It's very complicated.

37. You'd get a rise much .... if you worked harder. You'd get a rise very easily.

38. If you drove .... I would feel safer. I don't feel safe now because you drive fast.

39. This whisky is much .... than the one we make in our country. Ours is very cheap.

40. If you did that .... I would feel more confident. You do it too slowly.

Fill in the gaps 2

INFINITIVES WITH OR WITHOUT 'TO'

1. He's rich, but even so he can't afford ____________ a new car every year. (buy)
2. After some time I started ____________ what she really wanted. (understand)
3. He watched his wife ____________ up and ____________ to the window silently. (get) (walk)
4. I saw him ____________ the dog this morning. I'm beginning ____________ angry. (kick) (get)
5. I saw those two children ____________ your kitchen window pane and ____________ away. (break) (run)
6. I heard the referee ____________ his whistle and saw him ____________ for the dressing-rooms. (blow) (make)
7. When she had finished talking I started ____________ what she really wanted. (understand)
8. That boy is very good. He intends ____________ all the races this year. (win)
9. Mr Robinson, the manager allowed me ____________ and ____________ (get up) (go out)
10. She watched him ____________ the door silently and ____________ quietly. (close) (undress)
11. How ____________ you ____________ to me like that, young man? (dare) (speak)
12. The Evans let their children ____________ TV until midnight every day. (watch)
13. Jimmy's mother made him ____________ his face again this morning. (wash)
14. Mr. Brown, I regret ____________ you that your son has had an accident. (inform)
15. Give me the letter. Don't worry, I'll remember ____________ it on my way home. (post)
16. The teacher made little Jeremy ____________ to school last Saturday. (go)
17. Excuse me gentlemen. Could you help me ____________ the car? (move)
18. 'Don't forget ____________ the papers, will you!' 'Don't worry, I never forget ____________ any papers.' (sign)
19. He was so excited because she let him ____________ next to her. (sit)
20. It's a very nice play. I'd like to see you ____________ in a serious play like that. (act)

INFINITIVES WITH OR WITHOUT 'TO'

21. I like .... the washing and the ironing first thing in the morning. (do)
22. My mother prefers .... all those things in the evening. (do)
23. How dare you .... in here and .... me a liar, sir! (come) (call)
24. I felt something .... me on my head and everything went black. (hit)
25. You needn't .... anything yet. Wait until you get better. (say)
26. I dare not .... him up. I do not intend .... him up. (wake)
27. We managed .... the banner in time for the meeting. (finish)
28. We'll do our best .... it in time, but I can't guarantee it. (finish)
29. The two men were about .... the hotel when the police entered the building. (leave)
30. 'Did you see him .... the bill and ....?' 'Yes, I saw him .... and ....' (pay) (go)
31. Mr. Bronson recommended me .... the whole lot. He said it would be much cheaper. (buy)
32. Sorry, we can't afford .... the sitting-room every two months. (paint)
33. I was beginning .... very impatient. He didn't let me .... (get) (speak)
34. They couldn't afford .... cash, so they bought it on hire purchase. (pay)
35. That money allowed us not .... the bank for another loan. (have) (ask)
36. 'Does he like running?' 'Yes. He said he would like .... in the marathon.' (run)
37. Mrs. Robinson made little Jimmy .... with her .... to the teacher. (go) (speak)
38. I prefer not .... money rather than .... debts. (have) (have)
39. He intends .... the whole building and rent it in parts. (buy)
40. I won't forget .... it as soon as the shops open tomorrow morning.' (buy)

Fill in the gaps 2

COMPARATIVE STRUCTURES · AS .... AS · MORE AND MORE

1. Traffic on the roads is getting .... and .... every day. (bad)
2. The .... he bought it the .... he sold it. I couldn't understand it. (expensive) (cheap)
3. The whole affair is getting .... and .... complicated.
4. This man is making a fortune. He's getting .... and .... every day. (rich)
5. The .... you .... it the .... it becomes. (practise) (easy)
6. I am not .... rich .... you are, but I am .... intelligent .... you are.
7. That man is very ambitious. The .... he has the .... he wants.
8. Many other nations don't work .... hard .... we do in this country.
9. The .... money he had the .... the old man became. (mean)
10. You can eat and drink .... much .... you like. It's all free.
11. I don't know but this case seems to be becoming .... and .... (heavy)
12. Carmen speaks English .... and .... fluently every day.
13. The hole in the wall is getting .... and .... (big)
14. This man is very lazy. He works .... and .... every day. (less)
15. This girl is getting .... and .... every day. (pretty)
16. The airplane flew .... and .... above the clouds. (high)
17. My children learn .... and .... things at school every day.
18. The .... he bought things, the .... expensive he sold them. (cheap)
19. The .... I learn the .... I realize I know.
20. Sometimes it seems that the .... you run the .... you advance. (fast) (less)

COMPARATIVE STRUCTURES · AS .... AS · MORE AND MORE

21. You eat too much. The .... you eat the .... you get. (fat)

22. In summer the .... it is, the .... people drink. (hot)

23. In winter the .... it is the .... clothes people wear. (cold)

24. It was spring and the days were getting .... and .... (long)

25. Winter was approaching and days were getting .... and .... (short)

26. This boy of yours is getting .... and .... every day. (tall)

27. This little girl is getting .... and .... curious every day.

28. That athlete runs .... and .... every day. (fast)

29. Things are getting .... and .... every day thank goodness! (easy)

30. I'm afraid that things are getting .... and .... difficult as time passes.

31. Many countries are getting .... and .... every year. (poor)

32. I work 12 hours a day, but incredibly enough the .... I work the .... money I have.

33. Unfortunately, sometimes the .... you try to do something the .... you achieve.

34. Usually, the .... an athlete trains the .... tired he gets.

35. The .... the days, the .... time you can spend walking about. (long)

36. 'It's nice and warm.' 'Yes, the weather is getting .... and ....' (warm)

37. The .... the nights are the .... time one spends in bed. (short)

38. It's incredible, the .... I sleep the .... I get.

39. That girl's English is not .... good .... her brother's.

40. Usually the .... money people earn the .... they spend.

Fill in the gaps 2

YOU'D BETTER · I'D RATHER · IT'S ABOUT TIME

1. It's raining. We'd better .... to the cinema this afternoon. (go)
2. I know you can do it, but I'd rather .... it myself if you don't mind. (do)
3. I know I can go myself, but I'd rather you .... I think it'll be safer. (go)
4. 'It's about time you .... work.' 'Yes, it's about time we .... home.' (finish) (go)
5. We'd better .... if we want to arrive in time for the opening.' (hurry up)
6. My wife would rather we .... each other any more. (not) (see)
7. 'It's about time you .... home.' 'Yes, it's time I .... in bed.' (go) (be)
8. I don't like coffee. I'd rather .... a cup of tea if you don't mind. (have)
9. I'm very afraid of being alone. I'd rather you .... here with me. (stay)
10. You'd better .... a coat or you'll catch a cold. (take)
11. It's time the Government .... something about unemployment. (do)
12. I'd rather you .... with us. It is too dangerous. (come)
13. I'd rather .... too much work to do than have nothing to do. (have)
14. It's about time your son .... some work. He's getting very lazy. (do)
15. You'd better not .... me up when you come in at four o'clock in the morning. (wake)
16. You'd better .... a holiday. You look very tired. (take)
17. You can do it much better than Peter. I'd rather you .... it. (do)
18. It's about time you .... it to me. I haven't seen it yet. (show)
19. The house looks terrible. We had better .... the sitting-room. (paint)
20. It's about time you .... your homework, children. It's getting late. (do)

YOU'D BETTER · I'D RATHER · IT'S ABOUT TIME

21. I'd rather you .... with me. I would feel much safer. (go)

22. I'd rather .... to him myself. I still don't know what he wants. (speak)

23. You don't look very well. You'd better not .... to school today. (go)

24. It's about time your sister .... Look at the time. it's nearly 8. (come)

25. It looks like rain. You'd better .... an umbrella and your raincoat. (take)

26. I'd rather you .... to him yourself. You have more patience than I have. (speak)

27. If I went out for dinner I'd rather .... wine than beer. (have)

28. It's about time you .... dinner ready. it's already eight o'clock. (get)

29. You'd better .... to the bank this morning. They are closed in the afternoon. (go)

30. I'd rather .... tennis than golf, if you don't mind. I don't like golf. (play)

31. I'd rather you .... cash if you don't mind. I don't like cheques. (pay)

32. Are you all right? You had better .... You don't look well. (sit down)

33. It's about time you .... to the dentist. That tooth looks bad. (go)

34. 'I'd rather .... today than wait until tomorrow.' 'Well, I'd rather you .... tomorrow, actually. (go)

35. The water is very cold. You'd better not .... for a swim. (go)

36. They want to camp on my property, but I'd rather they .... here. I'd rather they .... by the river. (camp)

37. 'You had better .... the truth at the trial.' 'And you had better not .... anything about me.' (tell) (say)

38. I don't feel very well today. I'd rather you .... shopping. (go)

39. It's about time you .... me what all that is about, don't you think? (tell)

40. You'd better .... telling lies. Nobody will believe you, anyway. (stop)

Fill in the gaps 2

'GOING TO' FORM · WILL

1. This weekend I .... make a wardrobe for the children's bedroom.
2. 'When .... to see him?' 'I think that I .... see him tomorrow.'
3. '.............................. to the meeting tomorrow?' 'No, I don't think I .... go to the meeting tomorrow.
4. 'I .... take this box to the attic.' 'It is too heavy. I .... carry it.'
5. 'Do you think it .... rain tonight?' 'Yes, I think it .... rain.'
6. The weatherman on TV said that it .... rain tonight.
7. 'People say that they .... to get married soon.' 'Yes, and they .... probably be very happy together.'
8. 'When do you think you .... leave?' 'We .... probably leave tomorrow.'
9. 'I .... telephone my girlfriend.' '.............................. go out with her tonight?'
10. 'Do you think they .... come by plane?' 'No, they .... probably come by train.
11. 'Are you sure you .... post these letters?' 'Of course I .... post them.'
12. I .... to the Post Office. I .... be back in a minute.
13. We are really lost. I .... stop and ask someone the way.
14. She says that she .... be a jockey when she grows up.
15. I .... change. I .... be back in five minutes.
16. They .... build a motorway to the west, I think.
17. If you don't mind I .... marry your daughter in spring next year.
18. Look at those clouds! It .... rain any time, and I haven't got an umbrella.
19. If you invite them to the party we .... have problems. You can be sure.
20. 'We .... to Miami for our honeymoon.' 'I'm sure you .... have a wonderful time.'

'GOING TO' FORM · WILL

21. The car goes well. We .... be in Manchester before nine, I expect.
22. Look, little boy! If you do that again I .... box your ears.
23. 'My God! We .... crash!' 'Don't be afraid. I .... get you to London in one piece.'
24. If you come out for a walk you .... feel much better. You need some fresh air.
25. Our daughter .... have a baby in September or October.
26. 'Come to dinner, Jeremy.' 'OK, I .... bring a bottle with me.'
27. Look! My sister is wearing my coat! I .... kill the little rat!
28. Don't worry, I promise I .... pay you back as soon as I can.
29. 'Come out for a drink.' 'No, I .... miss my favourite TV programme.'
30. 'Darling, the Browns .... come for dinner.' 'OK. I .... be home in a minute.'
31. '.................... you give me a hand if I need help?' 'Yes, of course I .... help you.'
32. '.................... you get me a paper when you go out?' 'All right, I .... get you one.'
33. That man .... suffer for all he has done to our people.
34. 'You haven't written to your father yet.' 'OK, I .... write to him now.'
35. 'I .... not .... do the cooking today.' 'OK, I .... do it.'
36. 'This is a robbery. I .... not .... pay that bill.' 'Well, I .... pay it.'
37. 'Mum .... not .... do the shopping today. She's not well.' 'OK, I .... do it.'
38. 'I .... not .... pass my driving test.' 'Don't worry, you .... pass.'
39. 'I think I .... not .... run the marathon.' 'Don't be afraid. You .... run.'
40. '.................... to go to the concert?' 'Yes, we .... go together if you want to.'

Fill in the gaps 2

SO DO I · SO AM I · SO HAVE I · ETC.

1. 'I am learning French in a private school.' 'So .... I .'
2. 'They went to the bank early this morning.' 'So .... we.'
3. 'Your sister can swim very well, can't she?' 'Yes, but so .... I'
4. 'Peter can speak Italian very well, can't he?' 'Yes, and so .... his brother.'
5. 'We bought a new car last year.' 'Did you really? Well, so .... we.'
6. 'The Armstrongs went to Benidorm last summer.' 'Well, so .... we.'
7. 'These people earn a lot of money.' 'Do they?, Well, so .... we.'
8. 'We'll probably go to that place tomorrow night.' 'Oh, yes, so .... we.'
9. 'We buy the newspaper every day in this house.' 'Well, so .... we.'
10. 'I think that they will get tired soon.' 'Well, so .... you.'
11. 'This man is very clever, he speaks several languages.' 'So .... I'
12. 'I would go to Cancún on holiday if I could.' 'So .... I.'
13. 'I've finished everything on my plate.' 'Have you? Well, so .... I'
14. 'I think you speak too much and do too little work.' 'And so .... you.'
15. 'We'll sell our house as soon as we can and go away.' 'So .... we.'
16. 'We work 12 hours a day six days a week in this firm.' 'Well, so .... we.'
17. 'I have already written many books in my life.' 'Well, so .... I.'
18. 'I would go with them if I were younger.' 'Yes, so .... I.'
19. 'My brother will go to university this year.' 'So .... mine.'
20. 'My boss is at a fair in South America.' 'That is a coincidence, so .... mine.'

SO DO I · SO AM I · SO HAVE I · ETC.

21. 'My father was injured in the accident.' 'Was he? Well, so .... mine.'

22. 'Last night we went to the concert.' 'Did you? Well, so .... we.'

23. 'Our little baby is very good.' 'Is he? Well, so .... ours.'

24. 'We are going to the theatre tonight.' 'Are you? Well, so .... we.'

25. 'All my children speak Spanish and French.' 'Well, so .... ours.'

26. 'When I was a boy I could run 100 metres in eleven seconds.'
'So .... I.'

27. 'I have already bought today's newspaper.' 'Well, so .... I.'

28. 'I would like to buy a house near the river.' 'So .... I.'

29. 'I have been through a very nasty experience.' 'So .... I.'

30. 'The journey was very long and I stopped several times on the way.'
'So .... we.'

31. When I was a boy I could play for hours without getting tired.'
'So .... I.'

32. 'Our President speaks for hours on end.' 'Well, so .... ours.'

33. 'I like to drink a glass of wine with my meals.' 'Well, so .... I.'

34. 'I was wounded during World War II.' 'Were you? Well, so .... I.'

35. 'My son is much taller than I am.' 'Is he? Well, so .... mine.'

36. 'My children speak French much better than I do.' 'Well, so .... mine.'

37. 'I have already spoken to the teacher.' 'Have you? Well, so .... I.'

38. 'My neighbours are going to go to live in another town.' 'So .... mine.'

39. 'I have won the first prize several times.' 'Have you? Well, so .... I.'

40. 'I told my father about the journey last night.' 'Well, so .... I.'

Fill in the gaps 2

NEITHER · NOR DID I · ETC.

1. 'We didn't go to last night's concert after all.' 'Well, neither/nor .... we.'
2. 'The little boy wasn't very good.' 'Well, neither/nor .... the little girl.'
3. 'I'm sorry, I didn't think of that possibility.' 'Well, neither/nor .... I.'
4. 'Sorry, but I can't speak French.' 'Well, don't worry, neither/nor .... I.'
5. 'I won't buy it after all, it's too expensive.' 'Well, neither/nor .... I.'
6. 'Sorry, we never go to the theatre.' 'Don't worry, neither/nor .... we.'
7. 'He doesn't speak Spanish.' 'Well, neither/nor .... his wife.'
8. 'We haven't done anything about it yet.' 'Well, neither/nor .... we.'
9. 'I wouldn't like to live near the river.' 'Well, neither/nor .... I.'
10. 'I could never run the100 metres in 11 seconds when I was a boy.' 'Well, neither/ nor .... I.'
11. 'I wouldn't buy that house, it's too expensive.' 'Neither/nor .... I.'
12. 'I haven't bought the newspaper yet this morning.' 'Well, neither/nor .... I.'
13. 'They weren't injured in the accident.' 'Well, neither/nor .... we.'
14. 'We were in a hurry. We didn't stop in that village.' 'Well, neither/nor .... we.'
15. 'I wouldn't like to go through that experience.' 'Well, neither/nor .... I.'
16. 'I couldn't find another job in that town.' 'Well, neither .... I.'
17. 'I never drink wine with my meals.' 'Well, neither/nor .... I really.'
18. 'I can never remember people's names.' 'Well, neither/nor .... I.'
19. 'My father is afraid of planes. He would never fly on one.' 'Well, neither/nor .... mine.'
20. 'I didn't speak to the teacher last night.' 'Well, neither/nor .... I.'

NEITHER · NOR DID I · ETC.

21. 'We didn't go to the theatre last night.' 'Well, neither/nor .... we.'

22. 'I can't see the football match on TV tonight.' 'Well, neither/nor .... I.'

23. 'I don't like my maths teacher. He is not very good.' 'Well, neither/nor .... mine.'

24. 'Our children don't speak any foreign languages.' 'Well, neither/nor .... ours.'

25. 'I haven't done my homework yet.' 'Well, neither/nor .... I.'

26. 'The teacher told us to buy a dictionary but I haven't bought it yet.' 'Well, neither/nor .... I.'

27. 'I couldn't run very fast when I was a boy.' 'Well, neither/nor .... I.'

28. 'I wasn't even wounded in the war.' 'Well, neither/nor .... I, really.'

29. 'We don't spend very much in this house, really.' 'Well, neither/nor .... we.'

30. 'Jennifer is not very pretty, really.' 'No, and neither/nor .... her sister.'

31. 'We won't go on holiday this year.' 'Well, neither/nor .... we.'

32. 'I don't like going to pubs.' 'Don't you? Well, neither/nor .... I, really.'

33. 'I wouldn't like to live another life again.' 'No, neither/nor .... I.'

34. 'I am afraid I can't do this now.' 'Well, neither/nor .... I.'

35. 'I couldn't send my children to England last summer.' 'Well, neither/nor .... I.'

36. 'We won't be able to go there until next year.' 'Well, neither/nor .... we.'

37. 'Our daughter is not very good at sports.' 'Neither/nor .... ours.'

38. 'My brother won't go to university this year.' 'Well, neither/nor .... mine.'

39. 'My mother doesn't like shopping in that supermarket.' 'Well, neither/nor .... mine.'

40. 'I couldn't get to the meeting on time.' 'Well, neither/nor .... I.'

Fill in the gaps 2

REPORTED QUESTIONS

1. Yesterday a man approached me and asked me where ______ . (live)
2. An old woman walked towards the children and asked what ______ on her property. (do)
3. I had an interview for a job. The man in the office asked me ______ . (smoke)
4. The woman at the Welfare Centre asked the child if ______ breakfast. (have)
5. She asked me if ______ in the country much longer. (stay)
6. Peter asked his girlfriend if she ______ to the cinema. (want/go)
7. 'What did those men want?' 'They wanted to know if I ______ money.' (have)
8. 'What did that man want?' 'He wanted to know what time ______ ' (be)
9. The policeman stopped the car and asked me if I ______ a driving licence. (have)
10. I asked them if they ______ any relatives in this country. (have)
11. The Japanese tourists wanted to know where ______ (Post Office/be)
12. The little boy approached the ticket office and asked how much ______ . (the ticket/be)
13. The American tourist wanted to know at what time ______ (train/leave)
14. She wanted to know why they ______ anything about it. (not tell)
15. The teacher came towards us. He wanted to know what ______ (do)
16. He asked me many questions. He wanted to know how old ______ . (be)
17. The tax inspectors wanted to know if I ______ a work permit (have)
18. He asked me if I ______ to the party. I said I wasn't. (go)
19. I didn't know the opening times, so I asked them at what time ______ (open)
20. They wanted to know where ______ from. I said I was from Barcelona. (be)

REPORTED QUESTIONS

21. The policeman wanted to know if I .... anything during the night. (hear)

22. First my father, then my mother, asked me where my friend .... (live)

23. 'What did that man want?' 'Well, he only wanted to know how much the car .... (cost)

24. 'Those tourists wanted to know where .... the money. (can/ change)

25. The shop assistant asked me what .... .I told him that I wanted to buy some sweets. (want)

26. The strange-looking man asked the girl in the shop if .... computers. (sell)

27. The little boy wanted to know where .... video games. (can/buy)

28. The Japanese tourists wanted to know at what time .... (train/ leave)

29. The two policemen stopped my lorry and asked me how long .... driving. (be)

30. The Japanese officer wanted to know what .... (word/mean)

31. The inspector asked me if .... any children living with us. (have)

32. I asked the two Swedish tourists if .... Spanish. (can/speak)

33. In the interview they asked me if .... in working for them. (be interested)

34. I asked the two lost men if they knew where .... (be)

35. The two young men wanted to know where .... (Central Bank/be)

36. 'What did she want to know?' 'She wanted to know if .... again.' (meet)

37. 'What did you ask the ticket collector?' 'I asked him at what time ....' (train/arrive)

38. He wanted to know if .... in the compartment. (can/smoke)

39. 'He asked me what .... all afternoon.' 'I said I had been playing football.' (do)

40. The teacher wanted to know if .... my homework. (do)

Fill in the gaps 2

TO SEE · TO WATCH · TO FEEL · TO HEAR· TO LET · TO MAKE

1. Mrs Armstrong called the little girl and made her ______________ her hands and face. (wash)
2. 'Jennifer, did you see your brother ______________ this morning?' 'No, I didn't see him ______________' (go out)
3. I heard the rain ______________ down all night on the roof and I couldn't sleep a wink. (fall)
4. 'Don't let that horrible boy ______________ near you.' 'Ok, I won't let him ______________ close to me.' (sit)
5. 'Did you see your father ______________ in that light plane?' 'Yes, I saw him ______________' (land)
6. Well, I can't make him ______________ that if he doesn't want to, can I? (do)
7. Don't do that again! Don't let me see you ______________ that again, little boy! (do)
8. I watched him ______________ into that pub, and then I followed him inside. (go)
9. Dad, let me ______________ your car tonight. I am going to the discotheque with my friends. (use)
10. Don't make me ______________ that again, Mr. Brown. I hate doing that. (do)
11. 'Did you let little Jimmy ______________ the car?' 'Yes, I let him ______________ it.' (drive)
12. 'You didn't see him ______________ the letter up, did you?' 'No, I didn't see him ______________ up the letter.' (tear)
13. 'We watched them ______________ that TV commercial for hours. It was very interesting. (film)
14. Did you see those two policemen ______________ down the door and ______________ the house? (break) (enter)
15. 'Dad, let me ______________ with you on this business trip.' 'Sorry, I can't let you ______________ with me.' (go) (come)
16. 'Did you hear those hooligans ______________ in the street all night?' 'Yes, I heard them.' (shout)
17. 'Did you see him ______________ in the marathon?' 'Yes, I saw him ______________ for nearly three hours. (run)
18. 'Did you hear the teacher ______________ something about the holidays?' (say)
19. Mrs. Brown watched her husband ______________ quietly and ______________ for the door. (get up) (make)
20. 'Did you actually see him ______________ the letter?' 'No, I didn't actually see him ______________ it.' (post)

TO SEE · TO WATCH · TO FEEL · TO HEAR· TO LET · TO MAKE

21. He felt the knife .... through his clothes and .... his skin. (cut) (touch)

22. The two children could hear a dog .... in the distance. (bark)

23. I watched Macasso .... that picture for hours. I was fascinated. (paint)

24. Well, I think that she mustn't make you .... those things if you don't want to. (do)

25. OK, boys, let us not .... with this sort of thing. It is very serious. (play)

26. I watched these people .... that big hole in the middle of the road. (make)

27. 'Did you hear the band .... at the concert last night?' 'Yes, I heard them .... (play)

28. Yes, I certainly heard the roof of the theatre .... down. It made a terrible noise. (crash)

29. James, dear, come and watch these children .... football on the beach. (play)

30. 'Didn't you feel the needle .... your finger?' 'Yes, I felt it .... my thumb. (prick)

31. I saw the man .... into that pub and .... for a drink. (go) (ask)

32. You can't make people .... in the elections if they don't want to. (vote)

33. I heard somebody .... the door and .... the room. (unlock) (enter)

34. We could hear people .... in the distance. They were asking for help. (shout)

35. Did you see the firemen .... the window and get into the house? (break)

36. The traffic policeman made him .... the car and .... him. (park) (follow)

37. The four friends let the little boy .... them to the beach. (accompany)

38. She saw the thief .... the wall and .... into the garden. (climb) (jump)

39. Mrs Armstrong heard her husband .... in the dark looking for the light switch. (grope)

40. I could hear Mr. Bronson .... on the other side of the wall. (cough)

IF CLAUSES WITH FUTURE · CONDITIONAL

1. Look, the bus is waiting. If we run we .... it. (catch)
2. If all our papers are in order we .... immediately. (leave)
3. We haven't got any money, but if we had money we .... to Miami. (go)
4. I love her very much. If she wanted we .... married straight away. (get)
5. If you haven't got any money I .... you some until the end of the month. (lend)
6. I am sure that if he knew what really happened he .... me. (tell)
7. If it's foggy the plane .... probably .... diverted to another airport. (be)
8. If the weather was good the children .... and .... in the garden. (go) (play)
9. If it stops raining we .... for a walk in the country. (go)
10. If it stopped raining we .... for a walk in the country. (go)
11. If we need money we .... the house and the car. (sell)
12. If I see you around here again I .... the police. (call)
13. If I didn't go to the meeting my mates .... angry with me. (get)
14. If we left straight away we .... probably .... in time for the reception. (arrive)
15. If you stopped drinking a bottle of whisky every day you .... much better. (feel)
16. If you went to see that film you .... to sleep tonight. (be able)
17. If I won a lot of money in the lottery I .... a car like that one. (buy)
18. If that factory closes down many people .... their jobs. (lose)
19. If that factory closed down many people .... their jobs. (lose)
20. I am sure that if you try again you .... in the end. (succeed)

IF CLAUSES WITH FUTURE · CONDITIONAL

21. If you lived by the river you .... the boat race free. (see)

22. If I knew he had no money to live on I .... him some. (lend)

23. I am sure that if you study harder you .... all your exams. (pass)

24. You can be sure that if you studied harder you .... all your exams. (pass)

25. I know that if I married her we .... very happy together. (be)

26. If the police give him back his passport he .... the country. (leave)

27. If the police gave him back his passport he .... the country. (leave)

28. If you stopped wasting your time so much you .... better marks. (have)

29. Look, Jimmy, if you stop wasting your time you .... better marks. (have)

30. If you write to your friends more often they .... to you more often too. (write)

31. I am cold and wet. If I had matches I .... a nice fire. (light)

32. If I finish reading the book tonight I .... it to you tomorrow. (lend)

33. If the owner of that shop was a little kinder he .... much more. (sell)

34. We are all very tired. If we had a rest we .... much better. (feel)

35. If you do the shopping in that supermarket you .... a lot of money. (save)

36. If you took your shoes off when you got home you .... more relaxed. (be)

37. If you went to bed earlier you .... better in the morning. (feel)

38. If you do something for other people they .... something for you when you need it. (do)

39. Don't worry. If the baby wakes up before you come back I .... him the bottle. (give)

40. If I went to the butcher's I .... some bones for the dog. (get)

Fill in the gaps 2

PHRASAL VERBS

1. On our way here the car suddenly stopped on the motorway. It broke ....
2. Finally, after many months of tension, war broke .... between the two countries.
3. The meeting went on for hours. It didn't break .... until nine o'clock.
4. Please, bring me .... the books I lent you two weeks ago.
5. After the talks between the union leaders and the railway the strike was called ....
6. Just before the war all the19 year-old boys were called ....
7. After thinking about it for hours, they finally came .... the solution.
8. That little boy is a nuisance. he keeps cutting .... every few minutes. Tell him not to interrupt us.
9. He cut .... the meadow and headed for the little house near the river.
10. I feel like having something to drink. I could do .... a cup of tea.
11. In this country you can't do .... heating in winter. It's too cold.
12. Mr. Armstrong fell .... the trick and it cost him £100. He was very angry.
13. Attendance is falling .... at football matches, according to the Football Association.
14. The soldiers stood to attention and saluted, then, at the sergeant's order, they fell ....
15. He had lost consciousness, but now it seems that he is coming ....
16. I'm afraid we are running .... petrol. The car will stop any time now.
17. The old man lay in the middle of the road. He had been run .... by a car.
18. The expedition started off early in spring, but it soon ran .... difficulties.
19. Three prisoners have run .... from this prison so far this year.
20. Mr. and Mrs. Smith are looking .... a new house in this area.

21. Thank you for your letter. I am very much looking .... to seeing you again.

22. Will you look .... the baby while we go out for dinner tonight.

23. When the detective caught the criminal he turned him .... to the police.

24. The school teacher turned .... to be an old friend of mine.

25. When his grandfather died little Jeremy came .... a small fortune.

26. Your daughter does not take .... you in any way. She's very different.

27. The plane is standing on the runway. It's going to take .... any time.

28. The poor man took .... drink after his wife's death. That was two years ago.

29. This factory turns .... more than two thousand cars a month.

30. The policeman signalled us to pull .... at one side of the road.

31. After a long week of rain finally the sun broke .... the clouds.

32. She broke .... their engagement when she found .... he had been unfaithful to her.

33. Finally the company had to give .... to the strikers' demands.

34. The rotten cheese was giving .... a very bad smell. She threw it ....

35. The doctor told him to give .... smoking if he didn't want to run the risk of getting lung cancer.

36. You will have to make .... for the time you have lost if you want to finish the work on time.

37. They put me .... for the night during my visit to Manchester.

38. Little Lucy takes .... her mother, she has the same face.

39. I am sorry I was very rude to you. I take .... all I said yesterday.

40. Remember to take your hat .... when you enter the church.

Fill in the gaps 2

PREPOSITIONS AT · ON · IN

1. My mother got married very young. She got married .... the age of 19.
2. Your mother and I never go out .... night. We don't like it.
3. 'Are you going to take long?' 'No, I'll be back .... about five minutes.'
4. My father and mother always stay .... home .... the weekends.
5. We are eight brothers and we always try to get together .... Christmas day.
6. My grandmother had a long life. She died .... the age of ninety-five.
7. We got married .... 1962 and my first son was born .... 1963.
8. The two athletes arrived practically .... the same time in the London marathon.
9. My mother likes to get all her children together .... Christmas.
10. I like to go out to the disco with my friends .... Saturday night.
11. 'At what time do they open?' 'They usually open .... nine.'
12. My grandfather died .... 13 April 1966. He had a heart attack.
13. Get ready to leave, everybody. We'll be leaving .... a few minutes.
14. Don't worry. I'll be back .... Monday .... the latest.
15. 'When is Daddy coming back?' 'He'll be back .... two weeks' time.
16. Every year we have a party .... New Year's eve. We don't go to bed all night.
17. The plane is going to take off .... about six o'clock .... the morning.
18. In most countries people retire .... sixty-five. Few people go on working after that age.
19. They got married .... the evening, ... September 25th.
20. Mr. Jackson is always very busy .... the mornings. He usually works until very late .... night.

PREPOSITIONS AT · ON · IN

21. We didn't know what had happened .... the time of the meeting.

22. She will come back .... a few minutes with a tray full of sandwiches.

23. We last met .... January. It was .... the10th January to be exact.

24. He started school .... the age of five, and left .... the age of 16.

25. .... arriving at the office they discovered the burglary. The office was in a mess.

26. Mr. and Mrs. Taylor always go out .... their wedding anniversary.

27. We always put an index .... the beginning of all our books.

28. All the babies in the nursery began to cry .... the same time.

29. In this part of the country you can see millions of stars .... night.

30. I like to get up early .... Sundays to go running .... the hills.

31. Don't worry, the job will be ready .... a week's time. You can be sure of that.

32. All passengers should be .... time for the train. Otherwise they will be left behind.

33. .... hearing the news he dropped .... a chair and looked down .... dismay.

34. The price of telephone calls is going up again .... January.

35. World War I ended .... 1918, and World War II started .... September1939.

36. It's very difficult to get hold of those items .... the moment.

37. Many people go hunting .... the rain. I don't like going out .... bad weather.

38. .... my way here I saw an old friend of mine. We were together .... school.

39. He is better .... health, but still blind .... one eye.

40. He was dressed .... uniform. I was dressed .... civilian clothes.

Fill in the gaps 2

VERB + OBJECT + INFINITIVE

1. 'Shall I tell Peter to come to the meeting?' 'No, I don't want .... ' (he/come)
2. Your sister, Mary, wants .... next to her in the cinema. (I/sit down)
3. I told .... I didn't want to speak to him any more. (he/go away)
4. Your mother asked .... the tickets for the concert tonight. (I/buy)
5. He wanted your sister to go to the cinema. He wanted .... with him. (she/go)
6. They didn't want .... to their party. They don't like me. (I/come)
7. The sergeant ordered the soldiers to aim their rifles. He ordered .... fire. (they/open)
8. Your mother wants .... to school today too, little boy. (you/go)
9. My mum told .... early. That's why we came running. (we/come)
10. I want .... it at once. Do you hear? Is that clear? (you/do)
11. I don't want .... any longer than necessary. You can leave any time you want to. (you/stay)
12. I wouldn't like .... all your money. Don't bet on that horse! (you/lose)
13. Mrs. Briggs wanted the girls to play outside. She told .... in the garden. (they/play)
14. The teacher made .... on Saturday morning to do the exercises. (we/come)
15. 'Do you like that boy?' 'Yes, I let .... next to me during the church service. (he/sit)
16. The teacher made .... the exercise again. He said it was all wrong. (I/do)
17. I didn't see them leave the place but I heard .... the door quietly. (they/close)
18. I don't know why, but they didn't want .... to the party tonight. (we/go)
19. I asked .... with us a little longer, but they didn't want to. (they/stay)
20. My mother asked .... my face again this morning. She said it was dirty. (I/wash)

VERB + OBJECT + INFINITIVE

21. Do you really want .... ? or shall I stay with you tonight? (I/go)

22. Would you like .... to him? I will call that boy to my office if you like. (I/speak)

23. 'Did you tell .... ? or did he go away because he wanted to? (he/go)

24. Have you asked .... to the workers' meeting tonight? (he/come)

25. Mrs Millbank expects .... her every time he comes to London. (he/visit)

26. 'Have the children seen the film?' 'No, I wouldn't like .... it. (they/see)

27. 'Where are the children?' 'I asked .... to bed early.' (they/go)

28. He advised .... not .... the police. We had better keep it to ourselves. (I/tell)

29. The McMillans asked .... dinner with them on Saturday night. (we/have)

30. What do you want .... you? I don't know anything about it. (I/tell)

31. My boss, Mr. Peters, doesn't allow .... in his office. (anyone/ smoke)

32. 'Did you send the children to the park?' 'Yes, I wanted .... in the park. (they/play)

33. 'Shall I go with you?' 'No, I don't want .... me to the doctor's. (you/ accompany)

34. Children, don't go near the water. I don't want .... too far. (you/go)

35. 'Do they want to have it done?' 'Well, they didn't tell .... it anyway.' (I/do)

36. 'What did he tell you?' 'He told .... the doors and windows. (I/close)

37. My grandfather expects .... him every week at the old people's home. (I/visit)

38. I would like .... me to their party. I'd love to go to it. (those boys/ invite)

39. Do you want .... him about it? Perhaps he knows something about it. (I/ask)

40. 'Shall I buy you the paper on my way to work?' 'Yes, I want .... it for me every day, please.' (you/buy)

Fill in the gaps 2

PRESENT PASSIVE AND PROGRESSIVE PASSIVE

1. My father reads the paper every day. The paper is .... by my father every day.
2. My father is reading the paper now. The paper is .... by my father now.
3. My mother is washing the dishes now. The dishes are .... by my mother.
4. My mother washes the dishes every day. The dishes are .... by my mother everyday.
5. Politicians make many promises. Many promises are .... by politicians.
6. These politicians are making many promises. Many promises are .... by these politicians.
7. They are pulling down the building. The old building is .... down.
8. They pull down all the old buildings in town. All the old buildings in town are .... down.
9. The police take all the old cars off the roads. All the old cars are .... off the roads by the police.
10. They are painting the outside of the house. The outside of the house is .... at the moment.
11. They always paint the outside first. The outside is always .... first.
12. My mother sweeps the rooms every day. The rooms are .... by my mother every day.
13. My mother is sweeping the rooms at the moment. The rooms are .... at the moment by my mother.
14. This cat eats a lot of fish. A lot of fish is .... by this cat.
15. The cat is eating the fish at the moment. The fish is .... by the cat at the moment.
16. Mr. Brown cuts the lawn every Sunday. The lawn is .... by Mr. Brown every Sunday.
17. Mr. Brown is cutting the lawn at this moment. The lawn is .... by Mr. Brown at this moment.
18. This man translates many books. Many books are .... by this man.
19. This man is translating that book. That book is .... by this man.
20. This policeman arrests many criminals. Many criminals are .... by this policeman.

PRESENT PASSIVE AND PROGRESSIVE PASSIVE

21. The police are arresting those criminals at this moment. Those criminals are .... by the police at this moment.
22. Children break many toys. Many toys are .... by children.
23. Those children are breaking those toys. Those toys are .... by those children.
24. The maid cleans the windows every day. The windows are .... by the maid every day.
25. The maid is cleaning the windows now. The windows are .... by the maid now.
26. Those men are repairing the road. The road is .... by those men.
27. Those men repair the road very often. The road is .... by those men very often.
28. That thief often steals cars during the night. Cars are often .... by that thief during the night.
29. Look! A thief is stealing that car. That car is .... by that thief.
30. They are accusing the man of robbery. The man is .... of robbery.
31. They are making handtools for exporting. Handtools are .... for exporting.
32. They make handtools for exporting. Handtools are .... for exporting.
33. They kill many people in a war. Many people are .... in a war.
34. They are changing the wheel at the moment. The wheel is .... at the moment.
35. The men are calling off the strike. The strike is .... off by the men.
36. My mother paints the kitchen every year. The kitchen is .... by my mother every year.
37. They are painting the kitchen now. The kitchen is .... now.
38. This man is writing a book now. A book is .... by this man now.
39. This man writes a book every year. A book is .... by this man every year.
40. This centre forward scores a lot of goals. A lot of goals are .... by this centre forward.

Fill in the gaps 2

PRESENT PASSIVE AND PROGRESSIVE PASSIVE

1. That man in the black coat stole my car. My car was .... by that man in the black coat.
2. The men were painting the room. The room was .... by those men.
3. My grandfather wrote a book every year. A book was .... by my grandfather every year.
4. My grandfather was writing a book when I entered. A book was .... by my grandfather when I entered.
5. My mother washed the dishes herself years ago.
   The dishes were .... by my mother years ago.
6. My mother was washing the dishes when I arrived. The dishes were .... by my mother when I arrived.
7. Politicians made many promises in the old days. Many promises were .... by politicians in the old days.
8. Politicians were making many promises those days. Many promises were .... by politicians those days.
9. They were pulling down the old building.
   The old building was .... down.
10. They pulled down all the old buildings. All the old buildings were .... down.
11. They were painting the outside of the house. The outside of the house was .... at that moment.
12. They painted the outside of the house first. The outside of the house was .... first.
13. The maid was cleaning the rooms at that moment.
    The rooms were .... by the maid at that moment.
14. The maid cleaned the rooms every day. The rooms were .... by the maid every day.
15. This cat ate a lot of fish when it was little. A lot of fish was .... by this cat when it was little.
16. The cat was eating the fish when I saw it. The fish was .... by the cat when I saw it.
17. Mr. Green was cutting the grass when we arrived.
    The grass was .... by Mr. Green when we arrived.
18. Mr. Green cut the grass last Sunday morning. The grass .... by Mr. Green last Sunday morning.
19. Mr. Gibson translated this book. This book was .... by Mr. Gibson.
20. Mr. Gibson was translating the book when I entered the room. The book was .... by Mr. Gibson when I entered the room.

PRESENT PASSIVE AND PROGRESSIVE PASSIVE

21. Scotland Yard arrested many criminals last year. Many criminals were .... by Scotland Yard last year.
22. The police were arresting a criminal when we got there. A criminal was .... by the police when we got there.
23. Little Mary was breaking her doll. The doll was .... by little Mary.
24. Little Mary broke her doll. The doll was .... by little Mary.
25. My mother was cleaning the windows. The windows were .... by my mother.
26. My mother cleaned the windows last week. The windows were .... by my mother last week.
27. Some men were repairing the road. The road was .... by some men.
28. Some men repaired the road yesterday. The road was .... yesterday by some men.
29. A thief stole my car during the night. My car was .... during the night by someone.
30. A thief was stealing my car when I arrived. My car was .... by a thief when I arrived.
31. They were making TV aerials for exporting. TV aerials were .... for exporting.
32. They made TV aerials for exporting. TV aerials were .... for exporting.
33. They accused the man of robbery. Tha man was .... of robbery.
34. They were accusing that man of robbery. That man was .... of robbery.
35. They killed many people in the war. Many people were .... in the war.
36. They were changing the wheel at that moment. The wheel was .... at that moment.
37. They changed the wheels after10 laps. The wheels were .... after ten laps.
38. My grandmother painted the kitchen every year. The kitchen was .... by my grandmother every year.
39. My mother was painting the kitchen when I arrived. The kitchen was .... by my mother when I arrived.
40. The centre forward scored a beautiful goal. A beautiful goal .... by the centre forward.

Fill in the gaps 2

REFLEXIVE AND EMPHATIC PRONOUNS

1. Mr. Robinson's son killed .... in a motorcycle accident last year.
2. My skin is very delicate. I often cut .... when shaving.
3. He was a strange old man. He often talked to .... as he walked.
4. I always wonder how young people enjoy .... in noisy discotheques.
5. Be careful! That little boy is going to cut .... with that knife.
6. Little children can't dress .... alone. They have to be helped.
7. You are going to hurt .... playing on those rocks. Be careful!
8. One can't blame .... for everything that goes wrong around one.
9. People who play with fire finish by burning .... if they are not careful.
10. My grandfather often cuts .... when he shaves.
11. The young woman looked at .... in the front of a full length mirror.
12. Jimmy, you must wash .... every morning. Do you understand?
13. 'Did you enjoy ....?' 'Yes, we enjoyed .... very much.'
14. Please, look after .... when you are away from home.
15. Don't worry boys. Don't blame .... for what happened.
16. The children are having a good time. They are amusing .... quite a lot.
17. Get down from that rock. You are going to kill .... up there.
18. Don't let her blame .... It wasn't her fault, really.
19. Look, children, here are the cakes. Please, help .... Take all you want.
20. After several days, the fire eventually burnt .... out.

REFLEXIVE AND EMPHATIC PRONOUNS

21. 'Who gave you that medal?' 'Well, the King .... gave it to me.'

22. 'Who did you speak to?' 'I spoke to the President ....'

23. 'Let's paint the house ...., boys.' 'OK, let's do it ....'

24. 'Was the play good?' 'Well the play .... was not very good, but I liked the acting.'

25. 'Who told you that?' 'Well, Diana .... told me what happened.'

26. Charles .... doesn't think that he will pass the exam. He says it's very difficult.

27. 'Is it very difficult to do it?' 'No, you can do it .... if you want to.'

28. 'I like the diamond ...., but I don't like the ring very much, I'm afraid'

29. 'Who repaired the TV set?' 'I repaired it .... yesterday afternoon.

30. 'Who opened the door?' 'Mrs. Ferguson .... opened it.'

31. 'I want to see the letter ...., not the copy.' 'OK., here it is.'

32. 'Do you want some more fish? Help ....' 'OK., I'll help ....'

33. 'Will you post these letters for me?' 'Why don't you post them ....?'

34. 'Shall I carry the case for you?' 'No, I'll carry it ....'

35. 'I am not going to help you. You can do it .... if you want to.'

36. Peter and Mary are getting married in June. They .... told me.

37. The children .... can decorate the classrooms at Christmas.

38. The boss .... was very worried when I saw him this morning.

39. Four people were injured in the accident, but the car .... was not damaged.

40. The headmaster .... gave us the history lesson this morning.

Fill in the gaps 2

RELATIVE PRONOUNS

1. The funny man .... came last night is my uncle Charles.
2. These are the boys .... were with me in my regiment, in the army.
3. The people .... live in this area are very healthy.
4. That is the man .... you spoke to on the phone last night.
5. It was terrible. Nobody .... saw the accident will ever forget it.
6. These are the houses .... were burnt in the fire last year.
7. 'This is the man .... I belong to.' said the runaway slave.
8. Those are the children .... father is such a famous writer.
9. That is not the man .... I spoke to yesterday afternoon.
10. The dictionary .... I saw in the library is one of the best on the market.
11. That is the man .... the house belongs to. He is the owner of the house.
12. There is a young woman here .... speaks several languages.
13. The people .... houses were flooded are in the church at the moment.
14. Anyone .... saw what happened, please inform the local police.
15. I think that was the woman .... I spoke to on the phone last night.
16. That is the man .... wife has committed suicide this morning.
17. All the men .... robbed the bank have been arrested by the police.
18. That is the man .... I gave the parcel to. He is the one .... signed the receipt.
19. That is the little girl .... parents are so rich and live in that mansion.
20. The boys .... we travelled with, were American, I think.

RELATIVE PRONOUNS

21. The man .... I bought the car from, is very strange.

22. The workers .... he employs are very efficient and hard-working.

23. The house .... I have lived for so many years, is going to be demolished.

24. I know a lot of people .... lived in that area during the war.

25. This is the girl .... I want to get married to.

26. Those .... live in London are called Londoners. The ones .... live in Dublin, Dubliners.

27. That is the boy .... always wins all the races .... he takes part.

28. That's Robert .... wife works in my brother-in-law's office.

29. What's the name of the girl .... has just come into the building?

30. I don't like people .... get angry easily. They are very untrustful.

31. That's the girl .... cuts my hair at the hairdresser's, her name is Jane.

32. Those are the cars .... are going to take part in the race.

33. That's the old man .... goes jogging every day in the hills.

34. This is Mr. Jones .... you met at the convention last summer.

35. The man .... runs an advertising agency wants to talk to you.

36. The man .... you had an argument with, is at the door waiting for you.

37. That is the boy .... your daughter is love with, isn't he?

38. This is the person .... you were talking about.

39. That is the strange-looking man .... used to come to the department store every Saturday.

40. That is the sort of book .... I should like to read when I am on the beach.

Fill in the gaps 2

COMPOUND ADJECTIVES

1. There was a .... man at the door. He wanted to come in. (a man with good looks)
2. The shop assistant was a .... young woman. (a woman with lively eyes)
3. It was raining and she was wearing a .... raincoat. (a coat which protects one from water)
4. You can put your money here. This is a .... investment. (an investment free of tax)
5. Our daughter is a .... young woman. (a woman who behaves well)
6. A thin, ... woman, smiled at him from the door. (a woman with a flat chest)
7. My father was a frelance writer, he was a .... man. (a man who employed himself)
8. The people of this country are .... people. (people with their minds open)
9. A .... cart moved slowly along the path. (a cart drawn by a horse)
10. In front of the boys there was a .... avenue. (an avenue lined with trees)
11. Their wages are very low. They are very .... workers. (workers paid very badly)
12. A .... young man sat at the other end of the room. (a young man with his eyes crossed)
13. She went to the music department and bought a .... record. (a record that plays for a long time)
14. .... often come to this emigrant club. (people who are home sick)
15. The boss is very happy with Janet. She is a .... girl. (a girl that works very hard)
16. The man wore a .... suit with white stripes. (a blue suit of navy tone)
17. A .... old woman answered him from the balcony. (an old woman with a sharp tongue)
18. A .... young woman with blonde hair answered the door. (a young woman with blue eyes)
19. A .... young man walked towards him. (a young man looking very scruffy)
20. Edward Barkley was a .... old man. (an old man with a thick head)

COMPOUND ADJECTIVES

21. A .... young man approached her slowly. (a young man of six feet)

22. There was a .... walk to the house. (a walk of ten minutes)

23. The delegates attended a .... conference. (a conference of three days)

24. The woman had a nice .... baby in her arms. (a baby three months of age)

25. In a corner of the room there were six .... sacks of potatoes. (6 sacks of 80 kilos)

26. The whole family went for a .... walk. (a walk of two miles)

27. A dirty .... girl approached him. (a girl ten years of age)

28. We provide a .... service to our clients. (a service of 24 hours)

29. I would like 10 .... stamps, please. (10 stamps of five pennies)

30. I want 6 .... loaves of bread, please. (6 loaves of 50 pennies)

31. Give me 4 .... joints of lamb, please. (4 joins of lamb of 2 kilos)

32. They climbed an .... high mountain. (a mountain 8,000 metres high)

33. He owned a .... plot of land. (a plot of land of 5 acres)

34. We bought a beautiful .... car. (a car of two litres)

35. Mr. Armstrong was a heavy .... man. (a man of 14 stone)

36. They drank several .... glasses of beer. (glasses of half a pint)

37. I am very proud of my .... device. (a device for saving lives)

38. They lived in a .... building. (a building of a hundred years of age.)

39. All the delegates had a .... meeting. (a meeting of two hours)

40. She gave me a .... ruler. (a ruler of twenty inches)

Fill in the gaps 2

PAST PERFECT

1. When I arrived at the station the train .... already .... (go)
2. He didn't want to go to the party because he .... already .... dinner. (have)
3. When he returned he saw that the neighbours .... another dog. (buy)
4. When he opened the front door he saw that the house .... (burgle)
5. I was very surprised because the boy .... never .... before. (punish)
6. The questions that everybody was asking was: .... he .... from behind? (shoot)
7. Then they realized that the cat .... through the back window. (come in)
8. When I looked up I noticed that someone .... the window. (open)
9. All the children .... their homework and were in bed. (finish)
10. We .... at a party in London the previous summer. (meet)
11. When the old man returned to his hometown he noticed that the High Street .... quite a lot. (change)
12. When I saw the empty glasses I realized that they .... already .... there. (be)
13. Did you recognize the place? .... you ever .... to that place before? (be)
14. He was very nervous because he .... never .... in public before. (speak)
15. Sorry, I .... that there were people in the other room. (not realize)
16. I .... drinking the beer when the clock struck eleven. (not finish)
17. It was already ten o'clock and the train .... the station yet. (not leave)
18. After he .... reading the book he switched on the television. (finish)
19. He was very afraid because he .... never .... before. (fly)
20. My mother .... cooking all morning and she was very tired. (be)

PAST PERFECT

21. They were tired because they .... playing cards all night. (be)

22. After twenty years, things .... For example the Bingo .... (change) (close)

23. When he arrived at the meeting point his friends .... already ....(go)

24. It was strange because she .... never .... late for work before. (arrive)

25. He swore at the trial that he .... never .... that man before. (see)

26. She didn't know how to handle the racket because she .... never .... tennis before. (play)

27. He was told that his old friend Mr. Smith .... five years before. (die)

28. When she got to the supermarket, it .... already .... (close)

29. When he saw young David he realized that he was not a boy any more. He .... already .... up. (grow)

30. Mr. Armstrong wasn't very thirsty because he .... just .... a beer in the pub. (have)

31. He tried to get hold of the controls but he .... never .... a lorry before. (drive)

32. I found the old man quite changed. I .... him for years. (not see)

33. When he telephoned her she .... already .... out with another boy. (go)

34. He came late to work because his car .... on the way. (break down)

35. After he .... all the paintings he decided he wasn't going to buy any. (see)

36. There were cigarette ends in an ashtray. He realized that there .... people in that room recently. (be)

37. He was told that the grocer, Mr. Gibson, ... his shop. It was a supermarket now. (sell)

38. I didn't want to go to the cinema because I .... already .... the film. (see)

39. After he .... the window he opened the door of the room. (close)

40. When he returned to the village his old friend .... already .... (die)

Fill in the gaps 2

QUESTION TAGS

1. Jeremy, come here! You are a very intelligent boy, ... ?
2. Mary, you had a dog when you were a little girl, ... ?
3. I met your father and mother yesterday. You have a very nice family, ...?
4. If you don't mind, we could go to the cinema together, ... ?
5. You won't do anything without telling me first, ... ?
6. The Evans were in Italy for a few days last summer, ... ?
7. You weren't in Benidorm last summer with your family, ... ?
8. John, Mary! you ate all the cheese in the fridge, ... ?
9. You've got one of those little Yorkshier Terrier dogs, ... ?
10. Your neighbours, the Smiths, haven't got a black cat by any chance, ... ?
11. You'll come to the party tomorrow night, ... , Charles?
12. You won't go to the discotheque with those friends of yours, ... ?
13. If you knew what really happened you would tell me, ... ?
14. You wouldn't go away without letting me know first, ... ?
15. You haven't been to see the bank manager yet, ... , Mr. Davis?
16. 'They got lost on their way there.' 'But they had been here before, ... ?
17. He drove the lorry! But he had never driven a lorry before, ... ?
18. I know that you are learning French, but you can't speak it yet, ... , Mary?
19. Your younger sister Marian can speak Italian, ... ?
20. There are not many people at the meeting today, ... ?

QUESTION TAGS

21. This park is very dark. There are too many trees .... ?

22. Let's go to a Chinese Restaurant. You like Chinese food, ... ?

23. I believe that vegetarians never eat meat or fish, ... ?

24. You didn't come in time to see the newsreel, ... , Bernard?

25. You arrived too late to hear the President's speech, ... ?

26. You'll do what I told you yesterday as soon as you can, ... , Lucy?

27. You won't go to Jennifer's party next Saturday, ... , Charles?

28. You wouldn't buy that house if it was haunted, ... , Robert?

29. I suppose that you would tell me if you knew something, ..., Mr. Lee?

30. You haven't eaten all the food on your plates, ... , children?

31. You have drunk all the champagne in the bottle, ... , Margarite?

32. When you arrived at the rendez-vous they had already gone, ..., Mark?

33. The children hadn't arrived from school when I rang up, ... , Mary?

34. You could speak Chinese when you were a child, ... , Chang?

35. Your sister couldn't cook when she got married, ... , Johnny?

36. There isn't much coffee left in the coffee-pot, ... Mrs. Barrington?

37. There is still a lot of tea left in the kitchen cupboard, ... , Mum?

38. You made your own bed every day when you were in the army, ... Ernie?

39. You don't usually cook your own dinner, ... Mr. Longmans?

40. Well, soldiers are supposed to obey orders when they are in the army, ...

Fill in the gaps 2

IMPERATIVES

1. I love children. .... the children .... to me, said Jesus. (come)
2. Come on boys, ... a game of football on the beach, shall we? (play)
3. Hilda, can you do something for me? .... the ironing this afternoon for me, will you? (do)
4. '.................... what I told you!' 'No, I'll never forget what you told me today.' (forget)
5. Darling, ... all the furniture. .... the maid .... that. (not dust) (do)
6. Daddy, ... me .... the car, I promise I'll be very careful. (drive)
7. '.................... so fast, Johnny. We're doing over a hundred miles an hour. (not go)
8. ...., Mary. .... the maid .... that, it's her job. (not get up) (do)
9. .... to me, will you! .... that stupid attitude! (speak) (not adopt)
10. Children! .... in the sitting-room. .... to play in the garden! (not play) (go)
11. Well, boys. .... here. Now, ... about what we are going to do about it. (sit down) (think)
12. I don't like that place. .... not .... to that horrible place again, darling. (go)
13. We still have plenty of time. It's very early. .... another drink, shall we? (have)
14. They want to speak to me, don't they? OK, ... them .... to speak to me if they want to. (come)
15. 'I think that hooligan is coming for you.' 'OK, ... him .... He'll have a warm welcome. (come)
16. '.................... that tomorrow is Sunday.' '.................... I won't forget it.' (not forget) (not worry)
17. 'They are going to throw this old book away.' 'OK, ... them .... it away. (throw)
18. Please, ... me your problems. I don't want to know them. (not tell)
19. Mary, ... your sister to come at once. .... her .... her history book with her. (tell) (bring)
20. 'We are going for an excursion in the country.' 'Are we? .... my friend .... with us. (come)

21. Lucy, ... the children not to run up and down the corridor, will you? (tell)
22. Lucy, please, ... the children .... up and down the corridor. (not let) (run)
23. .... Jimmy to open the window. .... him .... the door too. (tell) (shut)
24. Come on, boys, please, ... me .... football with you. (play)
25. We don't want you here. .... with your friends if you want to. (play)
26. 'He wants to go away.' 'Very well, ... him .... whenever he wants. (go)
27. 'She wants to do it this afternoon.' 'All right, ... her .... it if she wants to.' (do)
28. 'It's raining cats and dogs.' 'Well, ... it .... as much as it wants to.' (rain)
29. ' .... us not .... today. It is pouring down. .... in. (go out) (stay)
30. Johnny, ... with boys, will you!. .... with girls. (play) (not play)
31. 'A lot of people are coming to this place.' 'Well, ... them .... if they want to.' (come)
32. 'Look at all those bees coming towards us.' 'Don't .... them .... you.' (sting)
33. ' .... so much, you'll be sick.' ' .... me what I have to do. (not eat) (not tell)
34. ' .... not .... yet. It's still very early. .... us .... a little longer. (go) (stay)
35. Mrs. Smith says that she is going to complain.' 'Well, ... her .... ' (complain)
36. 'Those two boys are fighting again.' 'Well, ... them .... each other if they want to.' (kill)
37. Darling, ... the children's beds. .... the children .... them, will you! (not make) (make)
38. .... that company, Mark. .... me .... you against those people. (not keep) (warn)
39. 'I think they are going to come by train.' 'Very well, ... them .... by train. It's safer.' (come)
40. .... silly. .... and .... me .... you a nice cup of tea. (not be) (sit down) (make)

Fill in the gaps 2

BOTH ...... AND · EITHER ...... OR · NEITHER ...... NOR

1. .... Peter .... Mary came to see me yesterday. They came together.
2. .... my father .... my mother speak several languages. They are polyglots.
3. If you want to go to Glasgow you can .... go by train .... by plane.
4. He is going to run .... in the marathon .... in the10,000 metre race.
5. 'I don't know whether to write or telephone.' Well, to be on the safe side you can do .... write .... telephone.
6. In this tennis club you can do one of two things. You can .... play .... watch.
7. I don't like those two. I trust .... him .... her.
8. I'm sorry, sir, but .... Mr. Gibson .... his secretary are on a business trip.
9. Look, Peter. This is no good. .... you tell him .... I will.
10. The two boys were quite normal. They were .... stupid .... clever.
11. Mr. Bronson is a man who mixes with .... the rich .... the poor. He's very friendly.
12. When you finish secondary school you can .... go to Polytechnic .... to University.
13. The director of this film is a man who can .... act .... direct. He's useless
14. She is an actress who works .... in the cinema .... in the theatre. Se's very versatile.
15. Those people on strike .... work .... let other people work.
16. Well, you can .... wait for him .... leave him a note.
17. .... my brother .... my sister speak a word of French.
18. If you choose from this menu you can have .... soup .... salad.
19. My father is a very healthy man. He .... drinks .... smokes.
20. Well, we can do .... actually, go to the theatre .... have dinner.

BOTH ...... AND · EITHER ...... OR · NEITHER ...... NOR

21. Nobody answered the phone. .... Peter .... Mary was at home.

22. The players of that team are very bad, they .... play .... let the others play.

23. People invited to the wedding banquet can have .... meat .... fish.

24. My girlfriend, Jennifer speaks .... Italian .... German, fluently too.

25. It was .... Diana .... her sister that answered the phone. It was an older woman.

26. 'How can we go to the beach?' 'Well, you can .... walk .... take the bus.

27. We can do ...., watch the telly .... play cards in the sitting-room.

28. Camels are incredible animals. They .... drink .... eat for weeks.

29. Go away from my property! .... you go .... I call the police.

30. He is a very good athlete. He does .... run .... jump.

31. He is illiterate. He can .... read .... write a single word.

32. It's an average family. They are .... rich .... poor.

33. Well, it's very simple, really. .... you do it .... I do it myself.

34. Well, we can do ...., actually, we'll do some business there .... sightseeing.

35. Well, all those men are .... male chauvinists .... rather stupid. I don't know which.

36. The building materials used in these houses were .... of bad quality .... very expensive.

37. Well, you can't come in. You can .... wait outside .... go home.

38. .... Charles .... his brother are intelligent enough to go to university.

39. Well, ... Johnny .... his girlfriend are studying to become doctors.

40. Well, ... you give it to me straight away .... I tell Mummy.

Fill in the gaps 2

THE PLURAL AND FEMININE OF IRREGULAR NOUNS

1. If you go to our attic you'll probably find a lot of .... running about. (mouse)
2. The earl and the .... of Essex are coming to live in that castle on the hill.
3. In English, the plural of foot is .... and that of tooth is ....
4. 'Did you have any money on you?' 'Well, I just had a few .... in my pocket. (quid)
5. In the factory where my father works there is not a manager but a ...., she's very young.
6. 'That's a very nice little dog you've got.' 'Well, it's a .... really, you know. We got her last week.
7. The bride was so beautiful at the wedding, and the .... was very smart too.
8. You wouldn't think that that young woman is a widow and the young man with her is also a ....
9. The crowd looked up and could see several .... flying in close formation. (aircraft)
10. In a distant field he could see hundreds of white .... grazing peacefully and bleating.
11. Neither my brother nor my sister is married. He is a .... and she is a ....
12. The little goose-girl was looking after several .... by the river. (goose)
13. .... live mainly in Scandinavia, although, you can also see stags elsewhere. (deer)
14. Most people are very unfair to .... really, you know. (mother in law)
15. Can you see that boy and girl over there? Well, they are my .... They are my brother's children.
16. I live in a boarding house. Mr. and Mrs Smith, the .... opened the boarding house twenty years ago.
17. 'I have two granddaughters and four grandsons.' 'So you have six .... ?
18. The two .... spent all afternoon washing the clothes in the river. (washer-woman)
19. All the .... of this sect are having a meeting this afternoon at Eaton Hall. (brother)
20. The transport company says that the .... have arrived at the warehouse this morning. (goods)

THE PLURAL AND FEMININE OF IRREGULAR NOUNS

21. Give me a couple of .... for my two children. A blue one and a yellow one. To clean their teeth.
22. Mr. and Mrs. Green are the .... of this book. They have just finished writing it.
23. This is the prince and that is the princess. They are the .... to the throne of this country.
24. Drop these two .... in the slot and the door will open. (penny)
25. That is my father's brother and his wife, John and Mary Stuart. They are my ....
26. I love the life in the Army. I think I'm going to join the .... when I am older.
27. 'This material is very good.' 'Yes, I like my tailor to use good cloth to make my .... (cloth)
28. My mother is going to buy a few yards of these two .... She likes these materials.
29. Many .... dropped a penny or two in the old man's hat. He was playing the violin in the street. (passer-by)
30. In that picture are the .... of this country with their three children, the prince and princesses.
31. 'Where is the cattle?' 'Well, all the cows and the .... are grazing in the field.' (ox)
32. I love fishing. That river over there is full of .... and .... (trout) (salmon)
33. Your boyfriend has left you? Well, don't worry, there are plenty more .... in the sea. (fish)
34. Good morning, ladies and gentlemen. Here's the eight o'clock .... There isn't much .... today. (news)
35. Come here everybody! I have a really good .... for you today! (news)
36. The inhabitants of this island are cannibals. They are .... They eat men.
37. Those three women over there make hats. They are .... or milliners.
38. 'In the last two years January has been a very cold month.' 'Yes, we have had two very cold .... in a row.'
39. 'Millions of pounds have been spent on the project.' 'Yes, five .... pounds was spent on it.
40. 'The dress cost two hundred pounds.' 'Well, two hundred pounds .... a lot to spend on a dress. (be)

Fill in the gaps 2

REPORTED STATEMENTS

1. 'I will go tonight', he said.

2. 'She is in America', his brother told him.

3. 'Tell my cousin that I'm not going.'

4. 'I'm not going to do it', he told me.

5. 'Write it on the blackboard', the teacher told him.

6. 'Sit down next to me', she asked him.

7. 'Don't tell anybody', she asked him.

8. 'This restaurant is new', he said.

9. 'Listen to me!' he said to her.

10. 'I don't like films', his grandfather said.

11. 'Can you lend me some money?' John asked his brother.

12. 'I don't feel very well', she said.

13. 'I have not stopped smoking yet', Peter said.

14. 'I am very tired', his son said.

15. 'I didn't buy it because it was too expensive', he said.

16. 'Go away', the old woman said to me.

17. 'Don't leave the doors open', he said to her.

18. 'Don't be late', my mother said to me.

19. 'I'm leaving you', she said to her boyfriend.

20. 'Sit down on that chair', the teacher said to him.

REPORTED STATEMENTS

21. 'I'll study more. I promise you', he said to his father.

22. 'I'll buy you sweets', she said to the child.

23. 'I like my new job', said Freddie.

24. 'It's my own fault', he recognized.

25. 'I've just heard the news', my mother said.

26. 'I haven't stolen the money', he said to the jury.

27. 'Father will come tonight', she said to the child.

28. 'I'll write to you as soon as I arrive.' she said.

29. 'My husband has stopped drinking', she said to us.

30. 'I'm going to join the army', he said to me.

31. 'Write to me', she asked him.

32. 'I'll arrive tomorrow', he said to her.

33. 'Sit next to me', he asked her.

34. 'We will go today', they said to him.

35. 'Have you finished writing the book', she asked him.

36. I'll tell you tonight', Mark said to him.

37. 'Type the letter', the boss said to the secretary.

38. 'Don't smoke in here', she asked him.

39. 'I don't want to go to the cinema', said his brother.

40. 'I have never been there before', he said.

Fill in the gaps 2

EMPHATIC DO · VERY · OWN

1. Mary, put this dress on! Yes, you .... look nice with this dress on!
2. 'Your daughter sings very well, doesn't she?' 'Yes, she .... sing well!'
3. 'You didn't see my brother yesterday.' 'I .... see him! He caught the10 o'clock train.'
4. 'You didn't tell me about that girl!' 'I .... tell you last night!'
5. 'You don't speak French, do you?' 'I .... speak French, and very well too!'
6. 'The cat didn't break the glass, did it?' 'It .... break it!'
7. 'Your boy doesn't behave very politely, does he?' 'He .... behave politely!'
8. Hello, John, how are you? You are the .... person I wanted to see.
9. He was playing with fire in the cellar and burnt his .... house down.
10. 'Your sister didn't come yesterday, did she?' 'She .... come!'
11. 'You didn't play football last Saturday, did you?' 'I .... play!'
12. Your sister doesn't speak Italian, does she?' 'She .... speak it!'
13. Don't tell me a pack of lies, will you! .... tell me the truth!
14. 'You didn't see Mary last night, did you?' 'I .... see her!
15. 'Children, come here this .... moment! You are to apologize to Mum for what you have done!
16. Sorry about that. I'm afraid it was my .... fault. I should have told you before.
17. 'You didn't buy the books, did you?' 'I .... buy them! I bought them in the morning.
18. I don't see him much. I .... see his mother occasionally, though.
19. 'Well, we must go!' 'Don't go yet. Please, stay a little longer. .... have some coffee!'
20. 'You didn't tell him what I said, did you?' 'I .... tell him!'

EMPHATIC DO · VERY · OWN

21. Look at that piece of furniture. That is the .... thing I was looking for!
22. 'May I have something to drink?' 'Of course, ... have some tea!'
23. 'The little girl .... look pretty today, doesn't she?' 'Yes, she .... !'
24. 'That old man is a chatterbox!' 'Yes, he ....speak a lot, doesn't he!
25. 'Why don't you do what my mother says? You are always annoying her.' 'Oh, ... shut up!'
26. 'I would like to speak to you, Mr. Naylor.' 'All right, please, ... sit down.'
27. 'Can you hear your daughter speaking French?' 'Yes, she .... speak good French, doesn't she?'
28. 'You didn't tell your father the truth, did you?' 'I .... tell him the truth.'
29. 'My boss always types his .... letters.' 'Does he? I always type my .... letters too!'
30. That son of ours already has his .... bike. Now he wants to have his .... car too.
31. 'He didn't take you to the cinema, did he?' 'He .... take me!'
32. 'I always cut my .... hair.' 'Do you? and how on earth can you cut your .... hair?
33. Jimmy, I want to speak to you at this .... moment. .... come here!
34. 'You didn't tell me anything about it!' 'I .... tell you!
35. 'You don't really like my sister, do you?' 'I.................... like her!
36. 'Look at that beautiful sky!' 'Yes it .... look as if it's going to be nice today!
37. 'You didn't see the play, really, did you?' 'I .... see the play!'
38. 'You don't really have a car, do you?' 'I .... have a car, and a very nice one too!
39. 'You didn't really go out with the beautiful blonde, did you?' 'I .... go out with her!'
40. 'They don't speak English yet, do they?' 'They .... speak English, and quite well too!

OTHER TITLES

Complementary books:

- Elementary Tests · 3 levels
- Advanced Tests · 2 levels
- Structured Tests · 3 levels
- Bilingual Phrases · 5 levels
- Bilingual Translations · 5 levels
- Fill in the gaps · 3 levels
- Guide to Prepositions (English to Spanish)
- Guide to Prepositions - exercises
- Guide to Phrasal Verbs
- Phrasal Verbs - exercises

Grammars:

- English Grammar · 3 levels

Pastimes:

- Didactical crosswords

Reading:

- Reading books
- Reading books with tape
- Bilingual reading books
- Graded reading - French

Textbooks:

- Stanley
- Stanley, book of exercises
- Stanley, Teacher's book
- On Second Thoughts (children)
- In the Third Place (children)

Others:

- Traveller's guide
- English - French - Italian - German - Portuguese

Business:

Bilingual Business Letters

- · English - Spanish
- · Italian - Spanish
- · French - Spanish